MW01616706

Becoming

A

Better

You

"Me vs Me"

Apostle Mandrell Aiken

Text Copyright © 2022 by Mandrell Aiken

All rights reserved. No part of this book may be reproduced, scanned, or distributed in any printed or electronic form or by any means without prior written consent of the publisher, except for brief quotes used in reviews.

Please do not participate in or encourage piracy of copyrighted materials in violation of the author's rights. Purchase only authorized editions.

ISBN 978-0-578-29657-9

Printed in the United States

I would like to dedicate this book to GOD, the Author and Finisher of my life. To my children Kaliah (Li-Li), Mandrell, Jr. (Dee), Keeon (Big Goose), KaiDarius (Deeda), and to my grandsons, Kayden and Kalial. To my mother, Belvion Aiken, and my deceased father, Raymond C. Aiken. To my brother Bishop Rico Aiken, Sr. I love you all unconditionally. To my High Calling Ministries Church Family, my true warriors, and the greatest church in the world, I love you to pieces and back together.

A special thanks to Elder Angela Clinkscales (Cuz) who labored and pushed me to get this book finished and typed, worked, prayed and everything else on my behalf to complete this task. I so you love and appreciate all that you do. To Prophetess Roberta Monroe, thank you for everything in every way and for contributing to and investing in me spiritually and giving in so many ways to help me to seal the deal on my endeavors. The best Intercessor in the whole world, ever. To my ride or die Overseer Elaine Wilson, you have been here from the beginning of it all, getting me through the toughest times of my life. Thank you for not giving up on me when I dumped my whole mess on you. You stayed right here until I got it together. You'll never know how grateful I am for that.

Lastly, to every person who gave it your best shot to be unforgiving towards me, and blamed me for everything, and decided to play the victim, you made me the victor and this book would not exist without your ammunition. Thank you for forcing Me vs Me!

Lastly to the greatest publishing company with the most amazing, sweet-spirited person that GOD could have sent my way, Dr. Lady Sonia Cunningham Leverette and the Hadassah's Crown Publishing Company. Thank you so much!

You force your
blinded behavior
you have accepted
on to other people
and don't see
anything wrong with
it at all.
~Apostle M. Aiken~

Introduction

First giving honor to God who is the head of my life and my everything, and I thank God for His son Jesus Christ, the Savior of all, and the precious Holy Spirit that leads and guides me every day. To be able to perform, fulfill, and do the things deemed necessary for God.

I want to say thank you to those of you who have purchased this book, *Becoming a Better You, Me vs. Me*. This book was inspired to be written by a message God had given me. During the course of teaching it, it became so radical and alive that the Holy Spirit led me to put it in a book to help hundreds, thousands, and even millions of people realize that there is an antidote to many of our self-struggles.

I am honored to be the one the Lord has chosen to share the revelations, teachings, and inspirations with you to help your eyes open to a better life, better results, and an awesome experience with yourself that you may have never had before.

This is my way of sharing with the world how to complete yourself, within yourself, for yourself so you can be better for others. So many times, in life we research our lives for answers, but we never get the solutions. There were answers, all answers. Beloved today, I want to share with you some things that God shared with me that changed my life, not just as an apostle or pastor, but as father, a person, a son, a friend, a brother, and anything else I need to be to those that look to me for help and guidance.

So again, I want to say thank you for your participation. I pray as we take this journey together in this book that you will see who you are and that you will be the best you, you ever been. In Jesus' mighty name. Amen.

Apostlc Mandrell Aiken

Becoming A Better You: "Me vs. Me"

Contents

Introduction		3
Chapter One	**Getting to the Roots**	13
Chapter Two	**Being True to Ourselves**	25
Chapter Three	**Unselfishly Discovering Ourselves**	39
Chapter Four	**Stop Fooling Yourself**	59
Chapter Five	**Finding Your Own Solutions**	75
Chapter Six	**Becoming a Better You**	89
Chapter Seven	**Becoming You, Grand Finale**	119

Getting to the Roots

Getting to the Roots

It is time to get to the roots of our lives and kill the curiosity. This adventure will be great and meaningful as we find answers for our questions instead of assumptions. Add branches to you roots. Discover you.
~Apostle M. Aiken~

Chapter One

To truly get to the root of who we are, we must start from the beginning. I had to start on November 26, 1973, the day I was born. I have no control over how I was born, but I cannot have full control over who I have become without the blessed opportunity of being born.

In the beginning stages of my life, I went on a roller coaster ride, even at an early age. Many people think that because you are young, you do not remember things, but it's when you are young that even negative things develop in your personality. A child may not understand exactly what their eyes witness to the point of being able to give it voice or clarity, but the imagery we saw as children can sometimes stain and scar us for a lifetime.

There were things I saw at a young age that caused me to become sheltered and even live in a shell. There are things I saw that were great, and there were things I saw that were conflicting. These things did not come from a certain person like my parents or family. It was a collection of environmental things that caused me to see things good and bad, right, and wrong, and I'm sure I am not the only one who has such a testimony. The fact of the matter is I must live my life in the realization of my experiences. Sometimes people think because they see you one way that that is the highlight of your life, when that is far from the truth.

I had amazing parents who raised us correctly. They fed us, took care of us, got us what we needed, took us places I thought we would never go, and they did things for us that most children do not get the benefit of having. We were far from wealthy or rich, but we were healthy, loved and had a desire for one another. Even in the brokenness, we found a way to survive as a family. My dad worked in a plant for a great deal of his life, as did my mother. I always saw my parents working hard to get what we have, and sometimes I even saw my dad cry in secret when he thought he was failing the family. I saw many arguments get stirred up from simply trying to survive.

I've seen lonely nights and lonely days, simply because we did not know what to do. There was no plan, just a fight for survival. This was instilled in me at an early age. It is very important that I make an awareness because even with bad things being experienced and seen, there are good qualities that come from experiences. There are also those that give us the strength to become, be, and become better. With that being said, I was introduced to ministry at a very young age.

My oldest brother Rico used to sing in churches and stand up on tables at the age of three years old. He would sing so hard and so wonderful that people would literately throw money on the table when he was singing. My brother was two years older than me, so even at the age of one I could remember marveling at the sight of him doing this, even though I did not have a full understanding of what he was doing.

A couple years later, my brother was always called on during Easter or special events for the youth to sing. This Easter my brother was not able to do so because he had chickenpox. My father was one who had a strong determination, so he looked at me and said, "Son, can you sing the song?" I remembered wanting that attention also. I told my dad I could.

My dad and I got ready and went to church and upon arriving, they scratched my brother's name off the program and replaced his name with mine.

I can remember even at the age of three or four years old my name being called to come and do what my big brother had done. Even at that young age, I can remember the knot that developed in my stomach for such a hard task. I remember the sweat running down on my back, and a church that was so small yet is seemed so big. I never asked for that assignment; I was only asked if I could do it. As any child wants to do to make their parents proud, I stepped up as brave as I could to do what my brother did flawlessly due to his repeated experience. I leaned on the wall of the altar and began to stand there. I remember looking at my dad and him saying to me, "Sing, Son! You can do it. Open your mouth and sing."

I began to sing this song very comfortably to the point that while singing, I was rolling around on the altar, examining all the Easter baskets that sat on it. I was still fulfilling the task at hand. That changed my life, and it was not until the age of forty-six years old that I realized I had taken on a major responsibility that a child should not have to take on. It wasn't to sing. It wasn't to be heard. It was to become what was necessary for someone else so that we could look good as a unit and bring disappointment.

After singing the song, many cheered, many clapped, many said, "You did a good job," but not one person came forth with one penny and threw it on the table. I didn't get the applause or attention that my brother did for doing the exact same thing that he did. It wasn't until the age of forty-six that I realized some resentment developed in my spirit as a child. I praise God that those feelings and emotions did not harbor to the point that they made me have any ill feelings toward my brother. He was my hero, and there was nothing you could tell me wrong about my brother, young or old.

Often times, I wondered why I didn't get the positive praises like my brother and many other people for doing a job well done. This became the story of my life. I received and accepted the responsibility of being the black sheep of my family, and I didn't even know what a black sheep was. I didn't even know one existed. I just knew I was different, and I was treated differently. I was received differently and my results from doing some of the same things my brother did were different.

As a result, I begin to live my life in the shadow of my brother and many other people. I was afraid to take the horns and lead. I was intimidated at a young age to always be told what to do but never stepping forward to do what I desired to do. This put a big dent in my creativity and my originality. It caused me to depend on others to guide me and lead me in every area of my life. Not just at church, not just in music, but even as simple as making a choice of what colors to choose from a crayon box in Mrs. Hutchinson first grade classroom.

As time went on but still at a young age, I began to see myself wanting to be loved and accepted as others were. I failed greatly because no one was imparting into me that my originality was okay. No one was telling me "You are who you are and it's okay to be who you are." My mama always told me she loved me and kissed on me. My mama had a relationship with me that made me feel special. I felt like the only person in the world who truly one hundred percent loved me divinely without any question was my mom.

Though I knew my father did, I only felt safe with the love of my mama.

The love I shared with my brother was superior. It never went anywhere, and it never costed any damage to who he was in my life. But unfortunately, it did cost me to see him as the better person. It brought some level of competitiveness to us that I feel invaded our love and trust to just be brothers the way we needed to be. Again, I thank God for not allowing the contamination to ruin the love, peace, and happiness I have for my brother.

Chapter one of this book is to help you understand it's okay to visit your beginning point, because that is the point that started everything about you. If you search hard enough, you will realize there are some things that made you who you are right now that you had no idea where your attitudes or behaviors came from. Many of us only deal with our present. We're too afraid to look back at our past and be honest with ourselves because it will mean letting the people who we trusted and loved know that somewhere along the line, you let me down. I made it, but you let me down.

We must know that it's okay to have that kind of honor and honesty about ourselves. We make ourselves victim to ourselves when we deny being honest about things that cause us to become who we are. Trust is now ruined when we get older. It was ruined when we were young and developing. Don't be afraid to visit your starting point because when we become in touch with our starting points and become original, we become one hundred percent real with how we existed. We will find a way to keep our existence alive.

Being True to Ourselves

The truth will make you free, so free yourself. We don't have to remain what we've convinced ourselves to be. Give yourself the gift of honesty.
~Apostle M. Aiken~

Chapter Two

In this chapter, we're going to discover some things that can help us be true to who we are. We must realize that we must be honest with ourselves. It's sad to say that it is easier for us to be more honest with other people about ourselves than we are with ourselves. Have you ever told a fib or a lie, and you told it so many times you started believing it yourself? I'm sure we all have dealt with this in some form or another. That sad case is when it comes to us as individuals. We have done this to ourselves so many times that we have started having faith and belief in a lie that seems so true and real because it's the choice we made. We want the choice we made to be accepted more than the truth. When we bring such behavior and beliefs in our lives, they damage us inside and cause us to compromise with ourselves in certain situations. When we depend on this lie that we have made truth, it causes us to have a portal that is easily accessible for others to come in and manipulate, use, or abandon us, and unfortunately even hurt us to the core. We accept bad behavior, bad relationships, and bad choices because we have lied to ourselves to the point the lie has become real. We will not allow ourselves to get rid of the lie. We explain ourselves to others to make it a truth, but at the end of the day we still know within ourselves we are living a lie.

When I was coming up as a child, my daddy told me one day that when you point one finger, there are three more pointing back at you. This is what happens when we make and pretend that it's something better within us than it really is. We point people to a false truth, which makes it a lie. We must accept the other three fingers pointing back at us telling us there's a reality in us that we are not confident with. We must understand that we must dig deep and find these things in us that we presented as false identity so that we will feel strong and superior against ourselves. We all have many enemies, but unfortunately the real enemy is us. We have allowed certain actions, situations, and certain relationship to cause us to falsify our identity. We try to bring hope to a fictional character instead of accepting the nonfictional life we really must live.

It takes more energy to keep up the unreal person than it does to go ahead and hurt and get over whatever we don't want to deal with. It takes more energy to be the real person we truly are. We begin to tell ourselves that this is how it's going to be instead of accepting how it really was. When we accept how it really was, it will hurt us. But facing that hurt will produce strength that will get us past what we dealt with. Any kind of imagery or imaginary thing that we develop will prove that it is not real.

The scriptures even tell us, "Cast down imaginations" because there is no foundation or true development in imagination. Many young children feel they are alone. Their minds develop imaginary friends or a presence that will be something mentally that they can connect to, in order to voice the true character they possess.

Maybe a little boy will say, "I have a friend named Tommy but only I can see him. He's invisible." Parents or people of intelligence will say, "He is not real." But if the truth is told, he is not real to us. He is very real to the little boy that made him. We have all made some imaginary friends, but we don't think they are imaginary friends because we look at these people every day. We talk to them every day. We can touch them every day, but the relationship we desire from them is far from what they are giving in return. That makes them imaginary friends. The difference is we have a friend we have chosen that has not chosen us.

The term "Best Friend" means you both agree that there's no friend better than you, and you're willing to give the same energy to each other in any circumstance. But when one person can say, "That's my best friend" and the other person says, "She's not my best friend," that only proves that you're truly not best friends. It proves that your friends with a connection may share variables and may share similarities. But it doesn't mean that you're the best at it because if you were truly best friends, you would both give one hundred percent to each other. Not one giving ninety percent and the other one hundred percent.

To truly be the best, you must give everything you have to it. So, we have developed imaginary friends in a real world because we choose friends who want to tell us the truth. We choose friends who will allow us to stay the same. We choose friends who will allow us to be wrong and tell us we are right. This makes them fake friends, which makes them imaginary friends. They are presenting an image to make you feel good, but it won't make you be better.

We must understand that we have to look to the core of our existence. We have to be honest with ourselves and go back as far as we can in our lives even to childhood, even to infancy, if there's a way of knowing and being honest with ourselves. I've counseled many people and I've asked the questions, "Who is your biggest problem in your life? Do you hate anyone? Is there anyone that just pushes your button?" Sad but true, eighty-five percent of those people said themselves, "I did not know how many people shout in church but hate themselves. I did not realize how many people fall prostrate before the Lord and cry during the whole service, just to get up and dislike who they are."

I'd not seen so many people in church who can present God correctly, preach the gospel, and rightly divide the word of truth just to go back into the pastor's study to transform back into the person they can't stand. My brothers and my sisters, this is a harsh reality, but we must face it if we truly want to be free.

"For what shall it profit a man, if he shall gain the whole world, and lose his own soul?" (Mark 8:23) I am not telling you not to do what God told you to do, but I am saying to let the altar call begin with you. Not to pray others free or to lay hands on others in order to feel you have accomplished something from the word. But to tell yourself that I need to be changed, that I to need the very word that I preach, that I too need to be delivered from me. I need to take responsibility from my own actions and quit blaming others when I made the choices. When we find this kind of honesty being registered in our lives, we're going to see different results come forth.

Your enemy's job is to take you out. Your enemy's job is to constantly aggravate and frustrate you. Your enemy's job is to make you feel terrible and to tell you that you won't amount to anything. If you are your own enemy, then it is so hard for you to move forward because you keep spinning your wheels wanting to be free but frustrating yourself at the same time. It only becomes aware to you when someone comes and does something to you that reminds you of what you are doing to yourself. Then you magnify their actions and empower yourself to be greatly disturbed, when they only came and revealed what you already possess within yourself. Therefore, it's so important to become a better you because it's okay for you to tell yourself you can be better, and you will be better.

It's okay to tell yourself you've made a mess of things, but you are going to fix it. It's okay to tell yourself you have caused a lot of problems, but you are going to solve them together. When you can face yourself and be real with yourself, you will be able to build a level of confidence to know that you can face who you are and become the person you desire to be, while gaining the courage to reject the person you chose to be. You are not imaginary; you are real. The blood is truly pumping through your body. You can move and you can access yourself, so use the good things that are within you to put the bad things to flight and become better.

You versus You. If you would focus on who

you are and not focus on the people around you, putting all your energy into making sure you're not your own problem, your results will be greatly changed for the better. But we must be honest with ourselves, and I repeatedly say this throughout the entire book. We must be honest with ourselves. We have trained ourselves to be okay with lying to ourselves. That's why when someone is mistreating us and treating us so badly and horribly, we accept their acts and actions because we have been doing it to ourselves for so long.

Your friends ask questions like, "Why are you going through this? Why are you so deeply involved with this," knowing they don't treat you correctly? It does not hurt nearly as bad as the treatment we give ourselves. That's the true answer. But we disguise it and camouflage it with an answer such as "I love them." That is not a wrong answer because the sad thing is, we do love those people more than we love ourselves. If we did not, we would not tolerate such actions so easily without opposition. So, it is very important that we make our minds up to be better to ourselves. The way to be better to ourselves is to be honest and point blank say we have told lies to ourselves. We have misled ourselves and we have brought some terrible choice to ourselves, trying to feel better and hide ourselves behind falsehoods and lies and treaties that are not healthy for our outcome in this life. These actions cause us to cling and latch hold to ill behavior versus resisting and know better.

Ending this chapter, I say it is okay to investigate your heart, mind, spirit, and soul, and say, "I have damaged myself." I'm alive. But I keep committing suicide to my emotions and to my reality with lies and with mischievousness to the point that I really think I'm okay because I'm doing it to myself. I'm not hurting anyone else, when this is far from the truth because when people don't get the best of you, they must get the worse you. You don't think you're the worse you because you treat yourself so badly. You have become so familiar with the bad of you, you don't think there is anything wrong with you. You force that blinded behavior on other people and don't see anything wrong with it at all. With that being said, throughout the remainder of this book, we will be talking about some things that will profitably help motivate you to reach inside yourself and most of all, forgive yourself. Second love yourself. Third be yourself. "You versus You!"

Unselfishly Discovering Ourselves

It's time to put on our glasses
and look through the lenses
of our lives and discover who
we were, who we are, and
who we can become.
~Apostle M. Aiken~

Chapter Three

In this chapter, we will be discovering ourselves from a very unselfish point of view. We have allowed ourselves to develop a defense when it comes to dealing with us. This defense even is used when it comes to us dealing with ourselves. We always want others to be in a place to understand who we are, why we are, what we are, and we even want them to understand why we make some decisions and choices even when they're bad. Sadly, it stands the same way when it comes to us even dealing with ourselves. Even writing this book, I must discipline myself to allow this literature to be about others but redirected to myself. When it comes to dealing with ourselves, me vs. me and you vs. you, we will find ourselves easily influenced to become wayward from the issues. Most of the time our brain will create or remind us of someone else that did the very same thing or even a greater thing to us than we have done to ourselves.

In this chapter, we will look at ourselves from two prospective: the outer us and the inner us. Most of us stop with the exterior part of us. We never ever dig deeper to discover what's really going on with the interior side of us. We know what we did to the interior side of us, 99.99 percent of the time it's hard to shift the blame or make excuses to blame it on others. So, we're going to look at this from both perspectives. Hopefully, we will be able to discover some things within ourselves that may be painful to do but truly necessary. It's so much easier to deal with another person because we leave that person with the full responsibility of dealing with themselves, and no matter what our decision is regarding their issues, we are not at fault for their choices. When it comes to making choices and decisions for ourselves, we are one hundred percent responsible for the choices. Whether it's right or wrong, good or bad, we are responsible.

We will look at ourselves from the exterior point that is very powerful when used correctly. I call this the "mirror theory." The mirror serves a great purpose. It reveals us as we are. The mirror is intimidating for most people because they cannot face themselves in the reality of who they are. The mirror theory will make you have to accept what you see because you cannot change what you see in that mirror by the mirror, only by the image it casts a reflection for. Have you ever stood in front of a mirror and saw what you see about yourself and say, "I have to do something about that. I need to make some changes. I've got to get rid of this gut?" But then we walk away and forget that we're even big because we have learned to live with the exterior. We don't look at ourselves much in the mirror because we are afraid that what we feel inside will be as ugly on the outside as it feels on the inside. We will look at a scar and we will point it out to others. But when we look in a mirror, we try to avoid what we already know because we must deal with the reality of what we see.

The mirror theory is the most important part of discovering who you are because it is who you are. You won't look in the mirror and see the woman you want to be. You want to see the woman you used to be. You want to see the man you chose to become. You want to see the man that made it this far. You will see the man who exists. The reality of your existence will be the reflection you see, and that my brothers and my sisters is who we really are. Whether we like it or not, whether we agree with what we see or not, the mirror with the right lighting will always and forever show you who you are as a person. You can suck in your gut, but it still exists. You can put foundation over your scars, but they won't go away. You can cover things about yourself you don't like, but they won't disappear.

We must learn to face the reality of who we are. This is a very hard thing for most women to do, especially women who have become mothers because they develop new identities from giving life. It changes theirs. Whether it's a stretch mark, whether it's a scar and in sometime cases, it may even be a cut, but that body you see in that mirror is what possesses the damage. The enemy and even we ourselves allow ourselves to see the negativity, the ugly, and the deformity we have accepted from our task in life. We have got to find a way to accept the existence that we have and know that we are not changed on the inside because of what exists on the outside. One of the plans of the devil and your enemies is to get you to see what they see in a negative way. So, the reality of this is most of us have been damaged in life by life even by people we love more than anything. This damage is to the point that we don't have the strength or energy in many cases, or even the desire, to take the risk of dealing with those things because they may cause us to be as broken on the outside as we are on the inside.

I encourage you today to see your truth and see the reality of who you are because there is nothing wrong with you. The mirror is a tool, not a remedy. Our minds use the mirror to look for negativity within ourselves. I would not even criticize that theory because it's a reality. But what we do with that reality is going to make us or break us from being who we are. If I have reached a point where I'm different from the person I used to be on the exterior, I need to encourage myself that I have been there. I have lived that reality and I can live it again with some changes. The change may not be what it used to be, but love it a different way so it will be a good thing versus a bad thing. We must understand that our design came from God. He is the author and finisher. He is the beginning and the end, and sometimes in His process, it causes things to change.

Remember Moses went up the mountain the way he was, but he came from the mountain transfigured. We must understand that even to do the will of the Lord and to do good things, it sometimes costs us to be transfigured. A sickness may cost you to take medicine that may put weight on you. We have to deal with the reality of that transition, but it does not change who you are. It changes your design, but you are still great even with the change. The mirror only displays the change of the exterior, but you still have ownership of the interior. We must understand that the mirror should not be blamed for what we present to it. It must see what you see, and it can't lie to you as we do to one another. The mirror has to be honest and say, "This is you; there is no undo button. There is no delete button, and there is no back button. It is who you are. Accept that. Don't be afraid of it because it is still you." We must understand that the mirror used as a tool will help us mentally, even emotionally repair areas of our lives that can cause us to be healed on the inside when the outside cannot be changed. It will push you to the inner parts of you that made it and are still surviving. You still win because you are still alive. Even with the change, you live.

My dad had to have his leg amputated,

which caused him to be unable to walk the way he was created. But it did not keep him from being mobile. It meant a different way to deal with the exterior of his existence. He was not able to look in a mirror and see two legs, but he was able to see the man that owned the two legs. He was remembered he was also the man who had brought himself this far with those two legs, normally or even amputated. He was also the man that would not allow the change to kill him. It was not easy. No one wants to become handicapped, but there's something greater than handicap. It's called life. Whatever and whoever came to cripple you and force you not to believe in yourself again, whoever came to tell you that you will never be better than you are only came to push you to a place to do things with your handicap. You must understand that my dad could not walk with the leg that he came with, but he was able to be mobile with the person he was.

Dad may have required someone to get under his arms and help him to the wheelchair, but he was able to move to one place to another because the exterior did not stop the heartbeat inside of him from living. He accepted his fate, loved God through it all, and trusted that God was going to send help for the exterior part of him. Even when his prosthetic leg was made, it became decoration. It was not salvation for my dad because he could not walk with it and use it the way he was supposed to. So, the leg would become a monument of survival to say to the world, "I'm changed, but I'm still the same."

Situations may have entered into your life to tell you there is no way. You may be changed, but you're still alive. And when you're alive, you can survive. There is a part of you that can still change everything about you when you look beyond the exterior walls of your existence. Let the mirror qualify you to be reminded that every scar, every wound, and every deformity is proof of what you can handle, not just what you've been through. And we understand the things we have accomplished are testimonies and not terrors, we will force ourselves to keep going and pursue greater for ourselves and not others.

The mirror theory, the powerful weapon to bring a reality of who you really are, is what it is. It is who you are, and it is what you have become. The awesome part of the mirror theory is it presents who you are, and it also presents who you can change even on the outside. I can lose weight if I want to. I can get color and dye my hair. I can get lotion and get rid of my ash. I can go and apply what's necessary to this temple so it can be more suitable for me. Whatever it takes for you to feel good about you, do it for yourself but not others. If your favorite color is red, don't wear a blue dress because other people say blue looks good on you. Do what makes you feel good about you. If your black suit is your favorite suit, wear your black suit. Don't wear the beige one because people said they like it better. We've allowed people to rule our territory and our choices too long, and we are helpless people because we allow what they say to dictate who we become. Get your life back, face yourself, and tell yourself what you're going to do to be a better person, to be a better existence, and see things change for the better for you. This is what happens when you face you.

Now let's deal with the internal part of us. Unfortunately, the greatest a mirror can be as a tool cannot complete everything wrong with you. We must understand there is another way that we must learn to see who we are. I call this the "X-ray theory." Many of us want to see what's wrong with us from the internal position with the external tool. The mirror can't show you what's going on inside of you. The mirror cannot project your emotions, your desires, your hurts, and your pains. It can only show you the scars that those things caused. Internal damage must be seen with internal tools; this is what we call the X-ray machine. The X-ray machine goes beyond the walls of existence. It breaks the border of the outer crust of you, and it illuminates what's inside of you. It reveals what a mirror will never see sometimes. A mirror can only see the results of what the inner things cause.

If you have cancer, you can't see it with a mirror. You can only see the results and treatment in radiation or surgery. If you have a brain aneurysm, you're not going to see it in a mirror. You may see a scar where you were cut open to remove something harmful. You need to understand that the things that are going on inside of you deserve a different kind of attention and approach. You cannot use the outer layer tools to deal with the inward parts that are broken.

You will never be cut open to see if you have cancer with today's technology. Medical professionals will use technology to see if something exists that requires you to be cut open. We've allowed too many people to put knives on us to prepare to perform surgical procedures that aren't necessary because the surgery they have prepared for is not our diagnosis. They're trying to figure out how to make you happy instead of finding out what made you sad. They're trying to see how to get you further along rather than realize that you are stagnant and can't go any further. We have put our lives in the hands of surgeons who are people who don't understand and allowed them to try and analyze us, discern us, and give us instructions in areas of our lives in which they are sick as well. We must know that before any procedure can be performed, we first must identify what area is damaged and what area needs to be pinpointed to make it successful. We must understand that the X-ray theory is for us to come to the light of truth and say this is the real problem. Can we trust anyone with this? No, we cannot. Yes, the Bible says, "Make our confessions known one to another," (James 5:16) but we must be careful who the "one to another" is because everybody cannot handle the inner part of their issues. They have already misled you with the outer problems. Do not trust them with the inner things because without your organs and your inner parts, the outer parts are totally unnecessary because you will not have life to live.

The outer parts will become a corpse that is ready for display at the mortuary, to be embalmed, dressed up, suited and booted for your final viewing. We must get to the root of our issues and deal with the inner vows and inner healing necessary for us to be free. No one knows better than us what's truly wrong with us. If you are honest with yourself, you will know that most of us will not tell the truth about us. We tell the part that will get attention from people, but we will not share the horror that allows them to know our weaknesses. We limit our weaknesses so we can feel strong. This type of healing only produces a stronghold that now needs spiritual attention as well as carnal and emotional attention.

I want to challenge you to please get under the X-Ray, see the truth about you. Allow it to prevail so that you can be healed for real. There are things in your secrets, thoughts, situations that no one in the world will ever know besides God and you. Even if you don't feel like you can tell anybody what it truly is, tell yourself enough to be honest so that you can face yourself. Tell yourself it's okay to be free from these bondages. It's time to have that conversation with yourself, not your neighbor, not your best friend, and in some situations, not even your own mom or dad. There are some things you are going to only understand about you, and it's time for you to face you. Tell yourself, I know what I put you through but the same way I got you in this I'm going to get you out.

The same way I got in just to find your inner parts, I'm going to help you heal. I'm going to play a role in your life and quit depending on others to fix us. It is time for me and you to face ourselves, and when we both become honest and real enough to know the help we need, we will go together so we both can be healed. I know you are saying, "Who is we?" It's the part of you that you have totally shut down and not permitted to live based on the things in life. The part that you have allowed to come in and force you to the ugly part of you. The good part of you that doesn't say anything anymore and says "whatever." The good part of you that doesn't have a vision anymore, that just accepts the reality of what seems. The good part of you that used to have a dream, but now you want to fade away in la-la land. Wake that part of you up so that you can face him and tell him, "I need you back" because I can't do this by myself. We're no good separately, but let's come together and let us reason together and become what God chose us to be spirit and soul, Kingdom and earthly, spiritual and flesh. Let's be the body that presents itself a living sacrifice, holy and acceptable unto God and ourselves. It is time for you to face you.

Stop Fooling Yourself

It's time to fool the foolish people who have been fooling you. Don't play the fool. Fool them with survival.

~Apostle M. Aiken~

Chapter Four

In this chapter, we're going to talk about how we have allowed ourselves to be fooled by ourselves. What I mean is that we have allowed ourselves to think because we've dealt with things. We're okay. Sometimes we must admit we've dealt with things inappropriately and the wrong way. Just because you do something does not mean it was the right thing to do. Just because you say something doesn't mean it was the right thing to say, it just proves you said a thing, or you did a thing. It doesn't make it right because you did it.

Most people are wrapped up in the

"dealing process" versus the "healing process." So, in this chapter, we're going to talk about the "dealing process" versus the "healing process" and the solutions that come from the choices we make. Let's talk about the "dealing process" first.

The "dealing process" is when we deal with the thing and then close the door to it. We say, "I dealt with it; it's over." We often find out this is far from the truth because it so continuously pops back up in our lives. We must get a mind that we are tired of dealing with the same things repeatedly. This is the easy way out; this is probably one of the most compromising ways of us dealing with dealings. Someone can do something to hurt you. You will go approach that person and say you will deal with it, but you want to say what's necessary. You'll just say something to feel good about doing something about it. But what you said won't change what happened because you only said words to feel good about doing a thing. This won't change the outcome. You never took away that power that person has because the words that you needed to say to them were never spoken. In other words, you may approach a person and say, "Remember what you said to me the other day? You so crazy, but that's alright. I'm good." When you should have said, "Remember what you said to me the other day? It really hurt my feelings. I went home and cried about it, and I prayed about it. I asked God to give me the courage to talk to you about it because it made me feel some type of way. I just want you to know it hurt me. I'm going to ask you to please not say or do those types of things to me again because I don't want to feel that way again. I don't want it to cause me to come out of character with you." That's a solution for your problem. That's an attempt of healing the situation.

Many of us say things to feel better and feeling better isn't always a good thing because it leaves us open to be hurt again.

Many of us use the "sweeping under the rug logic," which means we just sweep things under the rug to keep from dealing with them, giving them a solution, and bringing closure to the issues at hand. I must ask a serious question with that theory. Where is the rug on the floor? Where is the floor? In the house? So just because you relocated the problem, it still exists in the house. You just can't see it, but it still exists. You grabbed the broom when you should've grabbed the dustpan also. This is one of the greatest delusions when dealing with people. I don't feel like dealing with this right now, and we normally turn off thing that need to be turned on, walk away from things, and assume that they're okay because we did not deal with what we did not want to deal with. Later we realize they have only gotten worse or still have the same power and intentions they had when we should have dealt with them. Dealing with things inappropriately leads to mass destruction.

Let's look at "sweeping it under the rug theory" again. How much are you going to sweep under the rug before you realize it's time to move the rug? You keep walking over the rug, tripping up and falling because you would rather fall than get rid of things that keep causing you to fall and be broken. But we must understand that the more you put under the rug, the smaller the rug becomes. After a while, the rug will not be able to cover all those things because you put too much under it. It no longer is a rug; it becomes shelter for your problems. It was designed to lay, serve as decoration, maybe even wipe off people's feet and serve its purpose. Now you have caused it to become something else. Now it is a covering and even a better word for it is a "cover up" for things you chose not to deal with properly. Now the rug has elevated from the floor, and you say, "I must get rid of this rug and the things under this rug." This is the blindside for us when we move the rug, and finally we decide to deal with most of these things. If I started sweeping things under the rug in two-thousand fifteen and it is now two-thousand twenty, I don't have to deal with the thing from two-thousand twenty. I still must deal with and remove the things from two-thousand fifteen. This is what causes a major problem in our lives. Things that we dance around, move on from, and even go to church and praise God about them being over, still exist because they were not dealt with and removed, just replaced in a different location. These problems present other problems which now cause us to say, "I got to try to remember what was done to me five years ago and try to bring closure to it, and

I've had five more years of problems added to that." So, it is probably going to leave me in a place to be defeated because I can't get the full attention needed for what I swept under the rug. So just because you're dealing with things does not mean you are free from them. It just means you gave attention to them to feel better about not dealing with them for real.

The "healing process" is a totally different, and it is the logical way. A healing process means you don't stop until you get closure. A healing process says, "I'm not going to allow this to continue to make me sick. I'm going to get rid of it. If you consistently have headaches all the time, at some point you need to go find out why. If Tylenol and Excedrin do not relieve your headache, it may not be a headache that's the problem. Your headache may be a result of a real problem trying to force you to get to the root of what's really going on. But it's so much simpler to take pills to deal with than to think it may be something more to it.

Anything that lingers for a long time is a problem. If you did not invite it into your life as decoration, if it showed up on its own, it more or likely is a problem. So now you have to go to the doctor and say, "I consistently have headaches. I don't know why." They may take an X-ray, Cat-Scan or MRI to investigate the thing to see what's really going on. They may come back with a report and say they don't see anything, but at least it gives you peace to know that you have attempted to ensure that what you are healing from is truly a headache and nothing more. Doctors may say they see a blood clot on your brain, but the testing gives them a fair opportunity to fix a problem before it destroys you. You are not healed if the same thing you tried to fix keeps coming back to destroy you. That means you are "dealing" not "healing." "Healing" is a process in which we need to make sure we're getting the proper diagnosis and that we are taking the proper procedures to manifest a positive outcome rather than hiding the reality of what's really going on in our lives. All the while, we are shaming ourselves to a greater or worse problem. So, if the doctor sees a mass on the brain, it gives him a chance to cut the brain open, remove the mass, and sew you up so that you can be healed. It may cause a scar, but you will live to tell people why it was there. It's time out for us allowing other people to explain our wounds and our scars.

It's time for us to face the reality of who we are and give our own testimonies. There's nothing sadder than seeing someone have to explain the goodness that someone else has experienced. Though the words may be powerful and may still cause us to be excited, it's just something about it when the person who endured the problem or hardship shares what they went through and for others to see the expressions on their faces. Seeing the tears of joy that roll down from their eyes from becoming a survivor of a bad thing just pushes us to know that they are grateful. It's time out for us being to be hurt, broken, confused, damaged, and ungrateful. It's time for us who are broken, hurt, confused, and damaged with a testimony to say, "It did not destroy me. Because I went beyond the things that came to take me out, I dealt with the real things inside. I got properly diagnosed. I was honest with myself enough to allow myself to realize I needed help to be healed set free and deliver for real."

"He who the Son sets free according to the word of God is free indeed," according to John 8:36. This simply means that Jesus set you free and you are free indeed, but we have to understand the only way we can truly be free indeed by the Son of God is to first be free within ourselves. To allow him to free us, we must understand that he can only free us and make us free from the truth, not a lie. Many of us are so busy trying to be set free we can't be made free. Anything set free can be captured again, and anything made free gives you the experience not to be captured again. So, if you get caught, it won't be because you didn't know how not to get caught. You chose to get caught. We have allowed so many things in life to seem right to the point we never search for what's truly right. You may say, "I'll deal with it," but that doesn't mean that you will heal with it. We have allowed the things we deal with to be okay for us, but there are just some things that we deal with that will never ever be suitable for where we are going and who we truly are. We need to be healed. We need God to spiritually write us some prescription to set us free from these diseases of confusion, delusion, and hallucination that make us think we are okay. We continuously show we are not free. Things recycle in our lives to continually damage us. It's time for us to look at ourselves and say, "We got to stop this, we must lay this aside. We must lay this down; it is not suitable for our destination. It is not suitable for our survival. It is suitable for us to become kingdom minded."

It is not suitable for us to get away from the danger of our choices. It's time to lay these things aside so we can deal with what we really need to deal with. It is time to be healed from bad decisions. It is time to be healed from bad choices; it is time to be healed from compromising things that still present themselves as problems." Healing is the key to becoming a better you, so quit fooling yourself into believing that just because you dealt with a thing you are okay. You are not okay; you just made a move toward feeling better about things. If it does not get you now, it will haunt you later. So be real enough to lay yourself on the cutting board and let the things and procedures necessary be founded within you to heal your mind, heart, and spirit. You can become a person with a testimony and not a sad story that continually shows you are still sick.

Finding Your Own Solutions

SOLUTION

Definition

a: an action or process of solving a problem

b: an answer to
a problem : EXPLANATION

Chapter Five

In chapter five, we're going to talk about some things that will hopefully help you take an easier approach toward yourself. We want you to find a solution when it comes to you. Many people have given you answers when it comes to you and what you need or desire. But it's time for you to know what's best for you. All answers aren't solutions. If I ask you how many eggs make a dozen and someone says fifteen, that is an answer, but it is not the correct answer. It's just an answer. If I want a dozen of eggs to fit in a carton, I need to say twelve and twelve would be the solution, not just the answer.

With that being said, we have allowed

many answers from others to take root in our decisions. But it's time for us to make ourselves aware of what's best for us. We do that by coming up with solutions to our circumstances and not just answers. If we were to be totally honest, we would usually choose the best answer even if it's not the right answer. We choose the best answer for our circumstances, but that does not mean it's going to change anything. It just means it wasn't the best choice. It is time for us to use our experiences as lessons to mature us and not as lessons to destroy us. Many people use their experiences as excuses, but it is time for us to allow them to be lessons. When we learn the lesson, we can attain the blessing. We must understand we have to live our own lives, and we are in control of making those decisions. But those decisions need to be made by us for us so that we can be the best person for ourselves. And when we are the best person we can be for ourselves, we will be the best person we can be for others. It will cause them to appreciate who we are even more.

One lesson that I've learned in life is that the only person we should try to change is ourselves. We should try to be a better person today than we were yesterday. I don't care if you were great yesterday. Be greater today; take it to another level. Sometimes to be great we must be still. Sometime to do more and get more accomplished, we must do less. Sometimes to say a lot, we must be silent. We must make the best choices for us in this next chapter of our lives. We must understand that it's our duty and our responsibility to ourselves to be better people and stop depending on others to make the best choice for us. To do this, we have to want to be better than the person we are right now. We must want to make better choices for ourselves than we have made before. Sometimes, what seems like a bad choice to others is a great choice for you. Have you ever had someone trying to force you to like someone because they like them? Have you ever had someone to force you to make a choice or decision because it made them feel good? It's time for us to make the best decisions for ourselves. It's time for us to be in control of ourselves more than we have ever been. We can and will do that when we learn to like ourselves. We must desire to be better than we are right now.

At this moment as you are reading this book, you must decide you are going to be better than the person you are right now. To be better means you must learn to thrive in the wilderness; you must learn not to give up at every awakening moment. You must learn to celebrate yourself when others are trying to tear you apart. When others are trying to cremate you, you have to find a way to create from within you and live. You owe that to yourself; you do not have to accept the plans of others over yours. Take your time; make your choices wisely. Don't let anyone force you into your decision-making when it comes to you.

It's okay to encourage yourself, just like in the Bible when David was the king and he had led the men so diligently. When they came to a battle where they lost their wives, children, and family, they seem defeated. The very men that David had chosen wanted to turn on him, even stone him and kill him. This is what people tend to do to us when we tend to let them down, even after we make the choice and decision they encourage us to make. When it does not go the way that's suitable to them or when it's not appealing for them, they will turn on us, want to stone, kill, and watch us suffer. If you don't love yourself enough to stay in touch with yourself, you will even allow them to take you out with their words, deeds, and actions. This is why it's imperative and very important that we learn to identify with ourselves and realize we deserve to live, we deserve to make mistakes, we deserve to be forgiven, and we deserve to get up, too. What better person to tell you that than yourself?

Even when the men wanted to kill David and stone him, David had enough energy, confidence, strength and determination. within himself to change the fight plan. He took it from a flesh war to a spiritual warfare. When you read the scriptures, he even changed his attire. He took off his war clothes and put on his worship attire. When he put on his worship attire, the Bible says he encouraged himself in the Lord (1 Samuel 30:6). When we learn to change ourselves in God, we will stop letting ourselves down. When we change ourselves in God, He gives us the strength to look deep into ourselves and find that energy and life that are necessary to bounce back and continue to go on. David found himself within himself by giving himself completely to God and encouraging himself in the will of God and God's plan for his life, not the plan man chose to destroy his life. Many people run to you with great ideas so that they will have access to you. Not to push you forward and see you be successful, but they find a way to stay connected to you by continually bringing frustration and delay to your life. All good ideas are not bad ideas; they may be great plans that have worked for others, but they never benefit you at all. That's why again it's important to know who you are. Make your choice and accept your choices for yourself.

When I was married, many people were trying to tell me how to be married. Many men were trying to tell me how to treat my wife, and many men would tell me what would work in my home. Years later I found out that the very plan they shared with me didn't even work in their own lives, and they themselves ended up losing everything they had because the plans they chose weren't even their own. It was a plan passed down from someone else to them; it did not fit the criteria of their marriage. If we're not careful, we will find ourselves forcing people to accept the way we did a thing. That's not fair because it may not work for someone else. We must be in touch with ourselves to the point we trust ourselves. We must find purpose within ourselves that will cause us to lift our heads high and know that we are somebody and we are greater than what we chose. We must define who we are and erase the definition others have written about us in our lives. You do not win this battle by arguing with the competition or by going head-to-head with the people who don't believe in you. You win this competition by looking within yourself, encouraging yourself and telling yourself you are somebody. You are better than what you have even told yourself.

One way to deal with this is to compliment yourself every day. Every day you need to look at yourself and say something good to yourself. It's okay to look in a mirror and say something nice to yourself. This does not make you arrogant. It does not make you high-minded. It makes you confident in who you are. It's okay to say, "You did a good job on that meal today." It's okay to say, "You did a great job on that project at work; you worked hard. I'm proud of you." "It's okay to say you really are making it" taking care of your family. It's okay to say, "You really are doing a good job with the little bit you have." You can compliment yourself even physically. It's okay to look in that mirror and say, "Your eyes are beautiful." It's okay to say, "Your hair style looks immaculate." It's okay to say, "You look nice in that outfit."

Many times, we run to ask others because we like it, but we want to be more certain that they do. I've learned to outgrow what others think about what I like. So, if it's something I want to wear, I wear it. If it's something I want to do, I do it. When people come to me and say words like, "Man I don't like that outfit" it does not offend me because I know I did not wear it for them. I wore it for myself. When people come and say, "I don't like the way that you did a thing," it does not bother me because I know I did it the way I wanted it done. At the end of the day, I chose my choices over theirs. We must learn how to complement and give assurance to ourselves. This is totally okay; it does not make you better than others. It does not make you haughty. It does not make you belittle others. It just helps you pick yourself up. It helps you say, "You can do all things through Christ." It helps you say, "Greater is he who is in me, than he that's in the world." It helps you say, "I am a son or daughter of the Highest God." It helps you say, "God does love me even when others don't." It'll also help you say, "I love myself even when I didn't used to." Being true to you will produce a positive reflection of who you are to yourself first, then others get the benefits of loving the wonderful you that you are.

Becoming a better you starts with you and ends with you. It is you versus you, not you versus others. So, it's okay to dig deep and pull good things from out of yourself to tell yourself. You don't need an audience to know you're okay. You don't need someone to cosign your life after you make choices concerning it. You just need to know all is well with you because you made the better choice for yourself and that you do not depend on others to make those decisions for you. We don't want to become too cocky with our choices to the point we offend others, but we don't want to undermine ourselves to the point others get better results from us than we get from ourselves concerning us. It is okay to make yourself first and everyone else second.

Becoming a Better You

WHO ARE YOU?

Sometimes we're so busy knowing everyone else, we've become a stranger to ourselves. It's time to rediscover who we truly are and affirm our existence.
~ Drell ~

Chapter Six

In this chapter we will talk about some things that can possibly help you relate to the change that's necessary for your life. One thing we must understand is that there is something else on the other side of right now. Sometimes that something can be good or bad; it may be better or worse, but there is always something on the other side of right now. Many of us can never get to this place because we are so embedded in figuring out what has been. We are in a season and time of life where we grow and mature. We must come to grips with our future, which can be much more promising than our past, and in many cases, even our present. A lot of us cannot go forward because the past has baffled us so much that it's hard for us to strive beyond what we already know. This is one of the biggest deceptions we have come to learn for ourselves, to settle for what we know. Life is about changing. Life is about living. Life is about expecting better. In addition to having means to do better, doing better means to handle things differently on most occasions. Now, as we go forth discovering who we are, there are some things we must challenge ourselves to believe, deal with, and conquer. You must want to be more than the person that you are right now and know that there is a better person ahead for you, because that person is you. Sometimes we don't give ourselves a chance because we are so fed up with ourselves. That is often fed and even more triggered by being fed up with others. We must learn how to pull up cubicles and walls not to hide ourselves from the reality of life, but to seclude ourselves in order to strengthen ourselves.

When I worked in the mental health system, there was a place for the patient called "seclusion." That place was designed to keep people from harming others or themselves. Many times, we always try to get others to calm down, but how often do we tell ourselves to calm down? It isn't as bad or as serious as we try to make it out to be. Seclusion is a great place with the right mindset. It is a place to go to be prepared, not to hide and die. In this seclusion room, many times we would try to get the patient to just understand that their behavior was not acceptable or beneficial to them or others. It's so amazing how we can see the behavior in others that need to be changed but we're so blinded to our own needed changes because we accept them, and we want others to accept them too. This is one of the greatest tricks that is used against us, to be okay not being okay, to be wrong and not have to be right, because it's us and not someone else. We cannot deceive ourselves; we have a right and even a mandate to do better than we are right now. Even at this very moment as you are reading this book, your mind needs to reflect on what truly is and know it can even be better.

To be a better you, you must learn to thrive in the wilderness. Many of us want to come out of the wilderness never to remember it anymore. Unfortunately, some things in the wilderness are so harsh that we don't want to have to remember them. But if the truth is told, those are the things that make us and equip us to be better in our lives. We cannot erase them. They are a reality, but there is something better, and we are not the worst-case scenario. The wilderness is a place in which you must learn how to be content, how to go from place to place, how to avoid traps, how to endure. We are so overwhelmed by the wilderness experience at times.

When it comes to us, we have no fight left. Many times, we've fought so hard for others that we forgot to fight for ourselves. Think about how many times you have silenced yourself just to keep the peace? How many times did you just agree with something to keep from arguing? How many times did you just shut down so the other person would just shut up? Even though we seem to be gaining ground and winning, we're losing because the movie will still play when the pause comes off.

To truly benefit from these types of choices, we must face them, even if we don't like them. We must face them and come to a true reality of how to become a better person in them. Even if things don't change, at least it's fair now for you to know the truth about who and what you're dealing with. How many times have you trusted a person to change, simply because they said they would, and they showed you a day or so or maybe even a week or a month that change just to calm you down. But once they got you back to being complacent and settling for the lesser again, they go back to the same old ways and maybe in many cases, treat you worse. That is because you are relying on the power of another person to be your victory. This does not always work. In fact, it will always be a repetitious failure for you. We have got to find the strength within ourselves to be a better person. We have got to find the strength and courage to look at ourselves and know things will and can get better.

I am the one living this life. I'm the one who made the bad choices. I'm the one who has also made good choices, and the one that went too far. But I'm also the same one that knew sometimes to not go alone. This simply means that we have got to learn how to get ourselves a fighting chance in this fight.

When you fight another person, you give all you have to the fight because you don't want to be defeated and you can target the opponent easily. That same energy should be given to us not just to fight another person, but to fight for who we are as well. We have got to look at the enemy. Unfortunately, that is sometimes us. We must say the same way we wouldn't allow another person to hurt us or harm us, we will not allow ourselves to do it either. We have to see this even when it's us. We have got to come to grips with the reality and the discipline to know that we deserve that fight. We deserve victory even from the problems we have caused ourselves. We have got to embed that in our minds, that we have messed ourselves up even though we blame others. We have allowed ourselves to be belittled by the words of others, but we believe them. It is easily said, "People did this to me," but if the truth be told, who is the one that truly accepted, allowed, and permitted it? We did. Now, we don't like ourselves for not standing up against such accusations embedded within and principles that caused us to break our rule when it comes to us.

Here are some things we must do when it comes to us to better who we are. I have found out in my counsel to others that in becoming a better person, we have got to give ourselves a pass. We must be willing to be patient with ourselves, to be willing to listen to ourselves, to even be willing to talk to ourselves and say the truth about us to us, for us, and towards us.

One of the things I encourage people to do all the time when it comes to becoming a better person is to compliment yourself. Every morning before you go on your daily routine, take a couple of minutes to give yourself a compliment. If it's as simple as "you are beautiful today," if it's as simple as "no one can be better than you being you," or it may also be as simple as "I believe in you." These are compliments that will cause our minds and even our hearts and spirits to conquer things we normally accept. I often tell my people to read the Bible, get a scripture in you, pray, but if we're using these things as weapons versus tools, we may not still see success from what we're trying to implement. So, we must make these things a lifestyle. Nothing makes you feel better than someone coming up to you and complimenting you, even if it's as simple as "I like your hair." Even if it's as simple as "I like your smile." It is okay to be okay complimenting who you are when it comes to you. And so many times we expect people to give those compliments to us, but we don't feel like we deserve them. So, we put the battle and responsibility on another person to give us what we can give ourselves.

I'm preaching to the choir because for a long time, being a plus-size man, I would really feel a little distance when it came to my appearance. I would go to the gym and work out and still see no results. I would stop eating like I was just to find out it wasn't working, so my mind led me to the point of just accepting the fact that maybe this is just who I am and I'm going to be this way. But I had to come to realize that I was not fighting hard enough because I was not encouraging myself enough. So being a plus-size man, I had to go into the gym and do it because I deserve it. I have to not expect anything from others. I didn't do it to see how much weight I lost. My cousin who is a trainer told me stop trying to lose the weight and pay attention to the inches. Do your clothes fit better? Do your clothes feel better on your body? Are you moving better? Are you looser than you used to be? Can you bend over better? Stop beating yourself up with the results you see others having. Find the results that are working for you and apply them to your workout. Watch. You will enjoy exercising.

Now when I exercise it's a joy because I'm doing it for myself to feel better and to feel better about myself. Every step I make counts because I took the negative and made it a positive. I had to let myself know that the results I'm getting will work, but other people's results will never work for me. You must know who you are, what you are, and expect those things from yourself. And you must apply those things to yourself to get greater results. So, it's okay to compliment yourself and it's okay to say, "It's okay" because at the end of the day, it truly is.

Secondly, don't make excuses even when it comes to you. We're so used to making excuses to other people when it comes to what they should or should not do, or what we should and should not do. When it comes to us, we're good at making excuses to other people, but it's hard to make excuses for yourself when you know the truth about yourself. When you know the truth about yourself, it's hard to tell yourself, "I didn't do it because…" because we know the real story behind that because. Here is the reality; we must stop making excuses even when it comes to us. Instead of pointing fingers and making excuses about why you're not happy or successful in your life, own up to your mistakes and learn from them. When you do this, you will become a better person because you want work so hard trying to find fault in others. You will deal with the faults you find within yourself.

Stop making excuses is one of the greatest challenges that we can give our lives because it makes us better people. It brings us to a place to be at a sufficient standard and not have insufficient results. We make excuses because they seem to work. They may fool others, but they will never fool you. How many times have you called into work and told them you didn't feel well? Or how many times did you tell them you were going to be late because of a situation that you knew wasn't true? So just because the excuse has results does not make it good, proper discipline. It is a lie that works! In addition, it is time for us to even quit lying to ourselves because, we can tell the lie, but we also know we can't fully believe it. We know who we truly are even when others are fooled.

Next, practice forgiveness. We are so behind on this one thing that we cannot go forward in our lives. We must practice forgiveness. Forgiveness starts with yourself first. Forgive or let go of resentment; forgive to untie yourself from the negative experiences of your past.

Many times, we are so tied to our past that we cannot forgive ourselves. We must cut that rope, run far and as fast as we can from that past that lives in our minds and not our lives because when it's a part of our lives, it will hold us up. It will make us resent even who we are. Take time to meditate and give thanks for the wisdom and knowledge you have gained from your suffering.

Practice the "I forgive and release you policy." Many of us forgive, but we don't release. Do the same even when it comes to you. Forgive yourself and release yourself from that jail of unforgiveness so that your life can flourish, and you can use what you have gone through as an experiment to get past other things. Many of us say we forgive, but we wait to see if the same hurt or pain will show up again versus moving on in the opposite directions expecting a greater breakthrough and a better way of living. So, we waste our time wondering when it will happen again instead of thanking God we made it through it the first time and got past it. If we truly deal with it right even when it shows up again, our choices, consciousness, and even our input would be better. Because even if we fail, we will fail with knowledge this time because of experience. Stop holding people you say you have forgiven prisoners to your fear of forward progress.

Many of us hold people captive of the fear we have from going forward. It is impossible to go forward when connected so deeply to the past of unforgiveness. That's why it's important that we forgive ourselves and move forward and beyond these things that have cause us to be staged, and we can't go forward.

Brothers and sisters, as you read this book right now, I know there are thoughts, events, and people on your mind that you need to let go and release.

I love to fish for the sport, and many times I catch fish, take them home, and let them die. One day a guy asked me, "Why do you catch fish, take them home, and let them die?" I do it for the sport, not to eat. He said, "Well if you are going to do it for the sport, catch them and release them so that they can live, so that someone else can catch them for the right reason." You need to release yourself for the right reason, simply so you can move on life and be appreciated by someone else. We must understand in life that we must learn to forgive. Also, we need to learn how to be honest and direct with ourselves.

You have heard me use this word "honesty" several times while writing this book. That honesty needs to be applied to you even if the honesty right now is, "I hate you." Things that are true can be changed and the truth will make you free, but until we admit that truth, we cannot make that change. Learn to articulate your thoughts, feeling and ideas in an open and honest manner. Be real with yourself, be open with yourself, and even if you must go in a room and shut the door, talk to yourself honestly.

One of the greatness problems we have with ourselves is that we've lied to ourselves and others so much that we believe the lies. The lies have become a reality, that reality is holding us up, and we are failing to an untruth. Stop lying to yourself because it makes it so much easier to lie to others. The Bible teaches us that all liars shall have their part in the lake of fire. This doesn't mean if you tell lies you're going to hell. This means if you do not acknowledge God as the Lord and Savior of all, you're a liar. If you can't identify His way to be righteous and perfect, you're a liar. If you cannot identify that His way is the only way that will give us good results, you're a liar. In other words, if you cannot identify Him as the supreme ultimate GOD for who He truly is, then you are a liar.

Now as it comes to you, you have been lying to yourself. Are you truly who you know yourself to be, or have you become what people wanted you to be to the point you don't know who you are anymore? What seems to be drowning you in life and keeping you from swimming to a safe place? Why are you drowning yourself? Why are you not paddling? Why are you not kicking? Why are you not screaming for help when it comes to you? You don't have to die and stay under the water. Breathe and know that help is on the way. What lies and schemes have we ignored because we convince people to believe the lie and the deception so much that we let it remain a living lie. So, it keeps us from truly repenting to God and even ourselves. How many lies do you have living in your life right now? How many lies do you have causing you to be somebody you know you're not?

Guys often go tell other guys that they have slept with women they have not even touched to build their life to be better than it is. We have peer pressure and pressure from other people that causes us to start lying about things to build ourselves up to the character of the group of people we're around to pretend like we are somebody. Instead of seeing them as superior, you should see them as people beneath you, because when you must lie to make yourself be something, you're truly nothing at all. So, promise yourself you will stop lying to yourself and know it's okay to be you because there is no one just like you. But what makes it great is the honesty behind being who you are, not changing to make others understand you.

Be helpful. Be helpful to yourself and

others. This will be a great tool for discovering who you truly are. The more you help others the better you will feel about yourself and everyone around you. Help is a gift from God also that many people ignore because it does not do a whole lot of "I" appeal. We love to do things for people to see us and to promote us as someone powerful. Help can be quiet, simple but powerful. Help others and help yourself by giving yourself what you are begging others to give you, doing for yourself what you are begging others to do for you. When God has given you the ability to do it for yourself, live and let live even when it comes to you. Believe it or not, another thing that will drastically help us is to listen to others. Sometimes people tell us the truth about ourselves, but we ignore that truth because we do not like what we hear. How many times have you asked your friend a question and they gave you the answer you did not want to hear? You didn't want to believe it because it was not the answer you wanted to agree with. We have got to learn how to listen to others because they can truly help us when we pay attention.

Listening to quality people is one of the greatest things we can do. Being a good listener can change everything you need to know and witness when people come to you. Being a good listener can change your life in a positive manner, especially when you listen to someone who really cares and loves you. Realize that sometimes the honest answer, ninety percent of the time, is the one that will hurt you the most, but it is the response that you need. That's why we don't want to listen because we hate facing harsh realities. Always be polite when it comes to you and others. The way someone else behaves does not have to determine your behavior. Stop allowing people to do stupid things cause you to become stupid. Just because they want to argue doesn't mean you have to get in an argument. Just because they want to fight doesn't mean you have to put up your dukes. You can stand there and say, "This is not what I want to do, and this is not what I'm going to do simply because you want to do it." Never let someone else's behavior determine yours.

Being polite makes people feel good and honestly, it makes you feel good, too. So, it's okay to be cordial and loving. You will get better results. Be yourself, align yourself with valuable people and things. Align yourself with valuable beliefs. Quit listening to every wind and doctrine that comes along to try to identify with all these different logics. Establish your own identity and stop being a different person to please everyone except yourself. This causes you to let yourself down and eventually it will let those down you're fooling as well. Build your own courage and stop relying on others to have it for you.

Stop depending on everyone to pick you up when you have two legs to stand on for yourself. Make yourself happy; find another way to live and to be valuable in your own happiness. All happy isn't valuable. Earn to create boundaries. Do not compromise when it comes to you. Find your focus and direction again and give yourself another chance to reset your life. Do the things that you desire to do, most of all, the things that you desire to do to please God.

Whatever happened to us loving ourselves to be a better person for God? It is truly not about us all the time. Be open to change; it's okay to be open to change and sometimes, you have the change to change. Many times, we allow people to convince us to change and we will change, but sometimes you need to change back. Did you change for you or for others? Did you make something different because it was what you like or what others like?

Making changes for others will cause you to not like who you are because it causes you to compromise the truth about who you are so others will like you and leave you hating yourself.

Now it's time to face who we are, like what we like, know what we know and accept it. Try doing something that has always scared you or that you didn't try just because your mind was so sure you wouldn't like it. It's okay to taste something that you've never eaten before. It's okay to go to a place you've never gone before. You may find out it's the best place you ever went in your life. So, quit hiding in your fears of routine. It's okay to live outside the box.

When you're honest with yourself, you have no problem moving outside of your comfort zone because it causes you to say, "I don't like it." How many times have you lied to someone who brought you a meal simply because you were hungry, and you did not want to hurt them to the point they would not want to feed you again? So, you lied about something you know you truly didn't like. When you love yourself, it's okay to say, "I honestly did not like that, but my heart is appreciative of your jester. Please don't judge me by such." That will make you happy knowing you were honest with yourself; it will change things drastically. You may discover another way is better, another person is better for you, or you may discover they are or are not. But that is what makes you so amazing with change. It keeps things in proper perspective. This also allows you to grow because you experience something new even if you don't like it. You have the testimony of saying, "I tried that." If you tried and don't like it, it makes you certain and it kills curiosity. It gets rid of the "I don't know mindset," which can sometimes cause us to miss out on great things. It's better to know than not know in many cases. Being certain requires less energy than not knowing.

I remember when I was young and still holding on to some racism. A big part of that were white people different from black people as much as others made it out to be? In my high school days, I made it my business to see what was so different about a white girl as opposed to a black girl. I took it upon myself to kiss a white girl, not because I wanted to, just simply to see what's so different about the color of our skin. After kissing this girl and using her just to experiment for myself, I realized it was only another person I was kissing, and the color was not involved. How often have we torn our lives up over ignorant curiosities that cause us to be held up, undeveloped, and uncertain of how great something could or could not be? We must remove that challenge and discover.

Becoming a better person won't happen overnight, but it is possible. God can do anything, and He can change us in the twinkling of an eye. We also must believe in ourselves and know that all things are possible even when it comes to us. We have got to stop beating ourselves up to the point we feel like we are helpless and hopeless.

I hope this chapter has taught you to give yourself a chance. That is the whole purpose of this chapter. It's to tell you to give yourself a chance, to rediscover what you have forgotten, and that is you! You are who you are, and you will forever be who you are. Even when you change who you are for others, you are still who you are. And on that note, there's nothing wrong with who you are.

Becoming You, A Grand Finale

It takes courage to
mature and become
who you are really
supposed to be. Define
yourself. Do not accept
other people's
definition of you.
~Apostle M. Aiken~

Chapter Seven

In chapter seven, I want to address, in closing, how we must observe ourselves: with an open mind and an open heart of reality. Many of us have no problem addressing ourselves, but we have a problem addressing ourselves honestly with an open heart and an open mind to our reality. We have allowed ourselves to believe the delusions and lesser answers for our situations because it feels better. Many of us have started believing in lies because we know they are far from the truth. When it comes to who we truly are and how we really are, we still condemn ourselves with a lie because it feels good and better than dealing with the truth.

Though this may be a quick fix to make you feel better, in a lot of ways, it may seem like things are going to be better at the end of the day and definitely in the long run. It will come back to haunt you. One of the greatest tricks of Satan is to fool us into believing that we are not the problem, when we know we are. How many times have you deliberately planned a conversation you're going to have with a person in retaliation? How many times have you done things just to frustrate another person so that you can get their attention? Because you have no love for yourself or belief in yourself to think you can sit down and be genuine and express how you truly feel, you find opposition to be a tool or a weapon. How many times have you deliberately stayed gone so you can make someone else mad? How many times have you not spoken to them, knowing there was a necessary conversation to be held? Even though we sit and blame other people, when we dig to the root or the truth of the problem, it is us hurting us because we are keeping ourselves from valuable and in most cases, valid situations that we need to get past. But we allow ourselves to contribute our own emotions to believe we are okay doing what we are doing because it was done to us.

I've come to find out in my recent study of myself and my recent ways of being honest with myself, I can almost guarantee you that if you apply this to yourself, your results will be the same, if and only if you be really honest. The results are that you are a hundred percent the reason for the problem in your life, because at the end of the day you will have influence, and even with persuasion, the choice is yours. We have the final say and decision over what we do or what we do not choose. Though the influence may have had some key factors in making a choice, we are still responsible for that choice. We are so used to blaming people for our choices that we think it keep us from being responsible for our choices.

I can remember many times when I was in school, my dad would say, "Mandrell, why were you in class cutting up?" I always remember trying to use the influence of others or even stating that someone else was doing the same thing, just to find out that he did not care or share any responsibility in that statement. His words would always be, "You are my son. I'm only responsible for you and your actions, so whatever someone else done has nothing to do with you or this house. So, don't tell me what they done because they are not my child."

I have learned in my adulthood that this is still the same. How often do we blame other people for the choices we made and though there is a reality to what is being said, it does not justify the fact that we made the choice? So, we are therefore still responsible for the outcome of our choices, even when it was unintentional or mistakenly done. We are still responsible for the choice. If you are not drunk, discombobulated, or incoherent, then you cannot say someone else decided for you. We just must admit, "I made a bad choice," so we can feel better about any decisions and choices we make. Once again, that blame or responsibility must come back to you.

What you have read in this book so far can only be powerful and meaningful if you are going to apply the information to yourself. I've found in many conversations with people that it is so easy to detour from myself and see them and blame them. Many people don't want to talk about themselves, so they will always find a way to make the conversation about you. That way, they can detour the conversation and the accountability from themselves to you. Unfortunately, we do the same exact thing to ourselves as well. When someone comes to have a discussion with you, it is very unfair that you make the conversation about yourself and not them. They came to you to get an understanding about a problem they have with you. Somehow you start using "the vice versa or contrariwise" effect by saying you do the same thing, or you are the same way. You weren't the one to start the conversation to get closure, they did. But it is very unfair when people take over a conversation that they did not initiate.

At some point to deal with you, you are going to have to learn how to shut down and listen to the person that has addressed and come to you with an issue. Accept the fact that they love and respect you enough to do so, versus talking about you behind your back or shutting down. Listen to everything they have to say, and yes, I'm preaching to the choir. Listen to everything they have to say before you give any input or insight into the conversation. Take notes, jot down things, remember things, hear them out and sometimes even in doing this, you still must come back with answers because you are not in an appropriate place to give answers at that time. It's okay to say, "Let me hear what you have to say; I'll get back to you so you can give the best and most profound answer you can. Because in many cases we forget how we have done things, or I may have addressed the person's issues. We need time to get our thoughts together to give the appropriate answer and not just an answer that will make sense. The reason many things in our lives never get closure is because we don't give the appropriate answers, just the sensible answer. Sometimes the sensible answer is not appropriate because it's far from what we believe or think. When it comes to dealing with you, the one person you can lie to but it will never ever make sense is yourself. Other people may believe the lie, may accept it because they have no idea to know any different, unless there's obvious evidence that you are trying to trick them. The one person you cannot trick is you; you just must deal with the truth. You shame yourself by ignoring it, but eventually running back into it, based on the fact you know better and you knew better. You can't hide you from you, even when you're doing a good job doing it. You still know in your mind and conscious, "I'm fooling myself to believe this."

So, in closing, make sure you do right by yourself for a change by being honest. Remember, it's your story to tell. You can tell a chapter, or you can tell the whole book. You can keep the book closed and tell nothing at all. But the one thing you must do is to be real and honest if you decide to tell anything. If you're going to tell anything, let it be beneficial for your clear conscious. The last thing you need to do is continue to lie to yourself and try to fool yourself like you're somebody else. Be a better you by coming forward, facing who you are, giving yourself a fair shot at becoming something great, by being honest, responsible, and accountable to yourself, for yourself, with yourself, by yourself.

I speak grace and peace unto you, pray the blessing of God finds you, and I pray that on your journey to becoming a better you, you discover just how great and truly wonderful you are. I hope that you annul the plan for your life that you're not good enough by realizing it's been you the whole time, the good, the bad, and the ugly. It all makes up the character of a great you. Grace and peace to all, and God bless.

Message from the Author

First, let me thank you in advance for reading this book and allowing it to come to life in your life. Secondly, you're going to thank me for this book because it's going to help you become aware of how to truly move forward in your life and love yourself for real. This book will show you how to deal with the true enemy. It will carry you into depths to finally be true to one's self. You will come out victorious in your life with this book. It changed my life writing it, and I know it's going to change your life reading it. You will feel the presence of GOD as these pages come to life for your life. This is the 1st volume of amazement helping you become "A better you." Again, thank you not just for reading the book but for having the courage to finally face yourself.

Apostle Mandrell Aiken/Drell_Az_I_Am

About the Author

Prentice Mandrell Aiken was born on November 26, 1973, to Raymond and Belvion Aiken in Antreville, SC, merely as a man. At the early age of 3, talents were discovered within him starting with singing. It was at that time that it was revealed that GOD had gifted this young man with a GODLY purpose to serve HIM.

Apostle Aiken started playing the drums at the age of 6 years old, and he was self-taught. At the age of 11, he wanted to do more with his talents and gifts, so he gained interest in writing and playing more instruments. He wrote his very first song "Save Your Soul." Also, at this age he was taught by his older brother, Bishop Rico M. Aiken, Sr., to play the bass guitar. This brother duo joined their father and began a singing ministry known as Raymond Aiken and

Sons. This group later became known as the Aiken Family after GOD allowed the mother's work schedule to change, and she was able to join this powerful singing ministry.

On July 21, 1990, Apostle Aiken came to know GOD personally and became HIS child versus HIS creation. He went from being merely a man to being a man of GOD! Later in life, he found himself serving in many capacities of ministries, from directing choirs and being a part of other bands. He and his brother started several bands, such as The Anointed Ones, RIP, Reek & Drell, Drell & Prophetic. He is now recording artist of his record label and production company Hiya Call'N Productionz LLC, where Apostle Aiken is the founder and CEO.

Apostle Aiken later joined Holly Creek Baptist Church under the leadership at that time of Pastor Harris E. Clark. Clark helped him with his vision and he was taught and imparted with much spiritual wisdom and knowledge for ministry. He was involved with establishing the music ministry. He began the youth ministry and served as the youth director. He was ordained as a deacon in 1998. On

August 19, 2000, he was licensed in the ministry under

Archbishop Harris E. Clark. In 2002, he was ordained as an

Elder. Apostle Aiken was also appointed the Director of

Protocol for Kingdom Life Fellowship International under

Archbishop Harris Clark. He served faithfully until God

revealed a greater plan for his life.

In 2005, God gave Apostle Aiken the vision to establish

High Calling Ministries International. At that time, it was an

evangelistic ministry allowing this young preacher to travel

far and near preaching the Word and operating with his GOD

given gifts, sharing with many throughout the body of Christ.

Apostle Aiken later started the Experience Movement, a

peculiar chosen vision for the body of Christ which was

started in 2008. This movement consists of churches coming

together, restoring the body of Christ, preaching and

teaching the preparation of the Gospel and bringing souls to

the kingdom of God. After a major turn of events in his life that shook the man of GOD greatly, it was then he realized GOD had other plans for his journey.

In 2009, GOD led him to settle his ministry from evangelizing to becoming the pastor of the great church today known as High Calling Ministries International. Apostle Aiken began this ministry in his living room, and it has blossomed into a powerful miraculous church that is maturing and growing daily by the grace of GOD. On June 11, 2017, Apostle Aiken was consecrated to the office of the Apostle by the GOD appointed officiate, Bishop James Wiley, Jr. Chief Apostle, and Presiding Bishop of The LORD'S Churches of Deliverance Apostolic Inc. Shelby, N.C. On this day, he established his Apostle's Seal and accepted the call to be chosen as GOD'S Apostle. GOD has given him the vision to start the HOLY Movement known as the "5-Fold X Experience" to restore the church back to GOD'S original purpose and to unify the Body of Christ as one. HCMI serves as the headquarters of this movement.

On December 11, 2018, Apostle Aiken was dually consecrated as he received Apostolic Secession from the hands of his Spiritual father and covering Archbishop Harris E. Clark. This was after Apostle Aiken urgently desired to be aligned with his Spiritual father to secure proper order to his call and vision. Apostle Aiken has started and established many ministries with the HCMI vision, where there are intense teachings and even a Bible College in major progress. This ministry and vision are built upon GOD'S Word according to Philippians 3:14.

Apostle Aiken has accumulated some college credits, has had many teachings, and has attended numerous classes in the ministerial training field to enhance and further his gifts for the call of God. But what's important to him is he knows he's saved and chosen by GOD "to study to show himself approved. A good workman needth not to be ashamed." It is his will to see all the glory be given to his Father, GOD ALMIGHTY.

Apostle Aiken has most recently accepted another fate in his life, and that is to become an author and writer. He is the owner of Hiya Call'N Publicationz, LLC. He has written has published *Becoming A Better You: Me vs Me* in order to launch his writing career.

Beginning at the Patrick B. Harris Mental Hospital and concluding at AOP (Anderson, Oconee and Pickens) Mental Health, Apostle Aiken worked in the mental health field from 1997-2004. He decided to use GOD'S Spiritual gifts in combination with his mental health specialist experience minister to people through writing, helping them become aware of how to handle life's challenges. Dedicated to his writing career, Apostle Aiken already has two more books in the making.

This GOD chosen vessel, father, and business owner's journey is far from over but has already seen many accomplishments that don't come close to those promises and the vision that await his future. Ministry is not new to this

Apostle of GOD. It has been a part of his life since his existence in this world.

Apostle Aiken presently is a native of Anderson, S.C. where he currently lives. He has four beautiful children: Prentice Mandrell Aiken Jr., Kaliah Meochia Aiken-Crawford, Keeon Malik Aiken and KaiDarius Wilson.

Contacting the Author

Email: drellhcp@gmail.com

Website: www.hcmiprosper.com

Facebook: @ Mandrell
Aiken https://www.facebook.com/itzdrell

Instagram: @
drellhcpstyle https://www.instagram.com/invites/contact/?i=1
w9lxqxbjrmsq&utm_content=537qf9

Twitter: @
mandrellhcp https://twitter.com/mandrellhcp?t=8fxZ44Z7AdG
HD93FV4d5ew&s=01